10X GROWTH IN YOUR MEDICAL ONCOLOGIST PRACTICE

10X GROWTH IN YOUR MEDICAL ONCOLOGIST PRACTICE

HEMANG C. PAJWANI

PENDOWN PRESS
Powered by **Gullybaba Publishing House Pvt. Ltd.,**
An ISO 9001 & ISO 14001 Certified Co.,
Regd. Office: 2525/193, 1st Floor, Onkar Nagar-A, Tri Nagar,
Delhi-110035
Ph.: 09350849407, 09312235086
E-mail: info@pendownpress.com
Branch Office: 1A/2A, 20, Hari Sadan, Ansari Road,
Daryaganj, New Delhi-110002
Ph.: 011-45794768
Website: PendownPress.com

First Edition: 2021
ISBN: 978-93-91266-15-8

Layout and Cover Designed by Pendown Graphics Team

I dedicate this book to all Experienced and newbies Healthcare Professionals, those who wish, but hesitate to go for Digital Medical Practice.

CONTENTS

INTRODUCTION

A well-planned medical practice could work wonders that you can dominate, provided it is put together in a seamless manner . Trust me, I will discuss my experience...

Hello! My Name is Hemang Pajwani, an Instrumentation Engineer by education, an Entrepreneur by Profession - who has developed a software for the first time that may help Medical Oncologists to create BSA based prescriptions in 2 minutes. I live and breathe for simplification and assisting to roar Medical Oncology Practice and hope it will continue to provide measurable results on a regular basis.

Throughout these preceding years, I've successfully observed and developed my software which will help newbies or experienced Medical Oncologists to obtain additional information from their medical practice.

The journey up to now has been brilliant! You will be wondering why I'm sharing this Book when I possibly could have charged a handsome amount for the same. . After all, if you implement the advice shared in this book , you can make a real killing and flourish your medical practice in leaps and bounds.

One, being in love with software for Medical Oncology Practice, it breaks my heart to observe many Medical Oncology Practitioners abuse it.

So I want to place maximum Medical Oncology Practitioners on the path.

Two, I am struggling to share with everyone due to time constraints personally, so this Book is my surprise to the new and experienced Medical Oncology Practitioners to share some valuable lessons that I have learned during my journey as a software company.

I am hoping these knowledge bytes will steer you to the road of success with Medical Oncology Practice. So without further ado, let's explore All about the lessons I learned Dominating Medical Oncologists Practice...

Yours friendly, influential Medical Practice expert.

Hemang Pajwani

AT THE END OF THE BOOK YOU WILL COME TO KNOW

- Rules to create Ideal and Error-free Prescription.
- Some DOs and Don'ts for issuing the Prescription
- Points to be remembered when Verbal Prescriptions are issued
- Importance of Drug - drug interaction
- What is ICD - 10 and its benefits?
- Maintaining health records by you as well as your patients
- How can you and your patients opt for EHR?
- Great things about Digital Medical Practice
- Precautions to be taken, if you plan for Digital Medical Practice

ACKNOWLEDGEMENT

I am grateful to Sr. Natalia D'souza, SSpS (Pharmacy In-charge Holy Spirit Hospital, Andheri, Mumbai), who gave her time to read / edit my manuscript. Your honesty, suggestions and advice helped me refine ideas and approach throughout the creative process. This book is richer due to your contributions.

Knowledge Byte 1

RULES TO CREATE IDEAL AND ERROR-FREE PRESCRIPTION

According to guidelines Prescription size should be: Minimum size (a)14X21cm (A5 size) & (b) XI x XI cm size.

Each Prescription should contain the following points:

- Doctor's name
- Education Qualification
- Registration number
- Full address, contact number, email, emergency contact number.
- Date of the prescription issued
- Unique Prescription Identification number
- Patient's name
- Address
- Age, Gender

- Weight
- Rx superscription- Not a legal requirement but frequently used as a matter of practice. It originates from the Latin "Take Thou"
- Name of the medicine - write the GENERIC NAME IN CAPITAL, with the brand / company name in brackets. Strictly avoid abbreviations or scribbling the name of the medicine/s.
- Strength or Potency of the medicine.
- Dosage Form- E.g. DT or Tablet, or Syrup etc.
- Dosage & dosing instructions.
- Total Quantity Refill information - If the physician wants the prescription to be filled/dispensed only one time, he should mention "SHOULD NOT BE REFILLED" or "DO NOT DISPENSE MORE THAN ONCE" at the bottom of the prescription (or get it pre-printed on the prescription blank). If the doctor wants the prescription to be refilled, he should evidently write the true number of times the prescription ought to be refilled. This is very essential to deter patients from refilling (repurchasing) the same prescription again & again unless otherwise directed by the physician.
- Doctor's signature, with date and stamp.

*Image of the ideal prescription is on another page.

(It is important to follow the format to ensure proper use of drug, avoid and detect any forgeries)

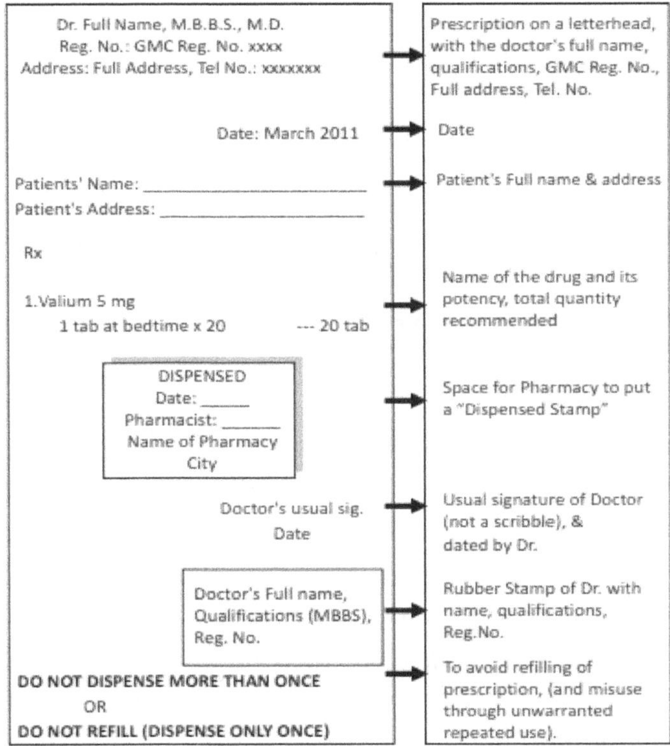

Ideal/Minimum Size of the Prescription Blank: 14X21cm (A5 size)

Knowledge Byte 2

SOME DO'S AND DON'TS FOR ISSUING PRESCRIPTION

- Complete prescription must be in CAPITAL
- Letterheads/prescription blanks should be kept securely to avoid misuse.
- Overwriting a prescription should be avoided. In case done, the doctor must initial each correction.
- Prescription whether typed or computer generated, must be dated and signed by the Doctor in blue indelible ink.
- It is illegitimate to permit nurses/assistants to create prescriptions/medication orders
- Doctors should always encourage pharmacists to contact them in the event of any problems/discrepancies/doubts/queries in the prescription.
- One should avoid having names of two or more doctors on the same prescription pad (even if it is a husband and wife team); more so if they belong to different specialties or systems of medicine.

- It is unethical for a healthcare provider to prescribe medicines for his/her own use except some OTC medicines. Self medication as an idea is to be discouraged.
- A doctor shouldn't use another doctor's prescription pad, even with his/her consent. Similarly a doctor should not allow another doctor to use his/her prescription pad.
- The doctor shouldn't write s.o.s. against any medicine. It is not an accepted abbreviation. The physician should use the correct abbreviation-p.r.n. (pro re nata) or the English equivalent-'as so when required'. In such instances, the minimum dose interval, the maximum daily dose and maximum duration and the maximum quantities to be dispensed, should be specified.
- Avoid unnecessary utilization of units.
- Doctors should be extra careful in prescribing habit-forming drugs or medicines with the prospect of misuse like sedatives, hypnotics, codeine containing cough syrups, Pentazocine, Buprenorphine, etc. Prescribers should inform the individual about their prospect of habit forming, in addition to the dangers of long lasting and excessive use.
- Doctors should be doubly careful on paper the potency & quantity of the drug/s. It is recommended to write the quantity in words. This is also to ensure that patients/clients do not manipulate the numbers.
- Write in bold "DO NOT DISPENSE MORE OFTEN THAN ONCE", at the centre or bottom of the prescription (considering that sometimes what's written in the bottom is taken off by the individual).

- Always write the potency for single ingredient drugs even when no other potency is marketed. You never know, when a new potency (higher or lower) would be introduced on the market.
- In case of mixture products, it is normally recommended to create the potencies of all individual pieces in order to avoid any misinterpretation at the pharmacy level.
- Doctors should avoid prescribing alternative medicines or other systems of medicine.

Knowledge Byte 3

POINTS TO BE REMEMBERED WHEN VERBAL PRESCRIPTIONS ARE ISSUED

In emergency circumstances if the doctor gives any verbal/ telephone orders regarding medicines to be administered to a particular patient the following should be remembered:

- The individual accepting the verbal order shall record and then read back the order in its entirety to the prescribing physician at the time the order is given, documenting that the order was "read back" (RB).
- Nursing staff shall tag all verbal orders with a "SIGN HERE & DATE" tag to alert the physician of the need to sign the verbal order after returning to the unit.
- Nursing staff is permitted to act after the verbal orders provided the orders contain the appropriate information.
- Verbal and telephone orders shall be initiated or signed by the prescribing practitioner as quickly as possible, not more than a day later.

- When the ordering physician is unavailable, it is acceptable for another unit team member or the attending staff to authenticate the verbal order.
- The attending nurse shall remind the treating doctor about the patient's known drug allergies marked with red ink on the patient's file to make sure that the patient will not receive that drug.

Knowledge Byte 4

IMPORTANCE OF DRUG-DRUG INTERACTION

Drug-drug interactions occur when two or more drugs react with each other. This drug-drug interaction may cause you to experience an unexpected side effect. For example, mixing a drug you take to help you sleep (a sedative) and a drug you take for allergy (an antihistamine) can slow your reactions and become worrisome.

After prescribing a drug, inform your patient about the following questions:

- Can an individual take it with other drugs?
- Should the patient avoid certain foods, beverages or other products?
- What are possible drug interaction signs, especially an individual should know about?
- How will the drug work in the individual's body?
- Are there more details available about the drug or patient condition (on the Internet or in health and medical literature)?

Inform Patient - how to take drugs safely and responsibly. Remember, the drug label will tell:

- what the drug can be utilised for
- how to take the drug
- how to reduce the threat of drug interactions and undesired side effects

Knowledge Byte 5

WHAT'S ICD - 10 AND ITS OWN BENEFITS?

The 10th release of the International Classification of Diseases (ICD-10) may be the latest edition (endorsed by the Forty-third World Health Assembly in 1990, and was in the beginning utilized by member states in 1994) to the system of codes that classifies every disease or health problem around the world. The previous edition was released about four decades ago and hence this release was seen as a sweeping change in the medical coding world.

ICD-10 provides a unique platform for practicing physicians and other healthcare professionals and is among the newest standards for clinical data, claims processing, clinical documentation, and public health reporting. The great thing about ICD-10 is that the transition commences with increased clinical documentation which permits physicians to investigate patient details, resulting in better care and coordination and thereby better outcome.

Top 8 Advantages of ICD-10 Implementation

Even though most healthcare providers have transitioned towards ICD-10, there are few who have not yet implemented it completely , or are in the process of doing so. In case you are not sure whether to make this transition or not here are few great things about ICD-10 implementation.-

1. **Fair Pay:** The brand new ICD-10 coding system is more granular in nature. This allows physicians to accurately report the complexity of the care provided and differentiate between chronic patients and the types who come for routine check-ups. Beneath the ICD-9 system this distinction would have been lost. Consequently, the customers can be charged as per the treatment provided, leading to better transparency in payment procedures..
2. **Greater Efficiency:** By implementing ICD-10, a huge amount of data will be produced and will be mined for the betterment of public health. It allows governments and healthcare officials to track and react to global health threats faster while comparing practices with the international community. Regions of injury research and trauma services analysis also have witnessed a marked improvement in classifying the sort of injuries and correlating them with the proper cause, treatment, and outcome.
3. **Lesser Fraud:** Adoption of ICD-10 will cause fewer fraudulent and exaggerated claims, which increases the price of medical healthcare insurance premiums. The conversion to ICD-10 shall eventually cause better patient care and more accurate reimbursement for providers as well.

4. **Improved Healthcare Quality:** With ICD-9, the key focus was on bettering reimbursements. However the ICD-10 coding setup supports a performance-based payment system that aims at returns instead. This changes how the healthcare functions currently and can enhance the overall quality of care being provided.
5. **Setting Health Policy:** Since the majority in the healthcare industry is using the ICD-10 code set, health officials can use the data to compare public health trends with global pandemics. This will help in setting-up better health policies across the world.
6. **Performance Monitoring:** The upgrade to ICD-10 will improve a provider's ability to monitor services and resource utilization, analyze healthcare costs, monitor outcomes, and measure performance. Greater detail on procedure types allows providers to judge their own performance in comparison with their peers, and take the steps needed towards improvement.
7. **Improved Quality in Clinical Documentation:** The ICD-10 coding system is indeed very much reliant on clinical documentation. Since a large number of diagnosis codes are incorporated into ICD-10, the precision of the codes is based on clinical documents. So, with the implementation of ICD-10, the standard of clinical documentation will certainly improve.
8. **Improving Relationships:** An upgrade to ICD-10 helps healthcare providers improve their relations with providers and vendors as well. Providers can partner with payers for coding improvements. Both payers and providers can collaborate and help to enhance the reimbursement processes, enhancing their income satisfaction and stream thereby.

Dos and Don'ts of ICD-10 Implementation

While ICD-10 is essential to be implemented, healthcare providers need to make sure that it is executed accurately, failing which can incur more problems to the practitioners. Below are few Do's and Don'ts of ICD-10 implementation:

Do's of ICD-10 Implementation

Conduct Training for the Coding Team

ICD-10 requires comprehensive workout sessions for the medical coders. Working out sessions must have case-based exercises which will help them think logically and act independently while coding.

Choose the Right Technology

Many healthcare IT companies have launched several tools to aid the ICD-10 implementation process. It is important that one chooses the correct tool which suits their requirement.

Be Aware of the most recent ICD-10 Updates

Updates to ICD-10 are being made frequently. so it is essential that you stay updated with the most recent changes happening in the market to stay up to date with the ICD-10 implementation.

Update Your Clients

Your clients should be regularly updated about the ICD-10 initiatives taken by you. Share your various plans, ideas, as well as drawbacks which will show them your commitment towards ICD-10.

Don'ts of ICD-10 Implementation

Don't do it in a Hurry

Plan a proper ICD-10 implementation process and work accordingly. The more it is delayed the riskier it is to work at the last minute. Let things happen as planned in order that you get enough time to fix any problems arising during the implementation and integration process.

Don't Leave Everything to the Coders

The ICD coding system demands a lot of groundwork to be done before implementation. The ICD transition should be a combined effort of the Transition management team, IT team, and the Medical billing team.

Knowledge Byte 6

MAINTAINING HEALTH RECORDS BY YOU AS WELL AS YOUR PATIENTS

A precise written record detailing all areas of patient monitoring is important, not merely because it forms an integral part of the provision of care or nursing management of the patient, but because it also contributes to the circulation of information between the various teams involved in patient's treatment or care.

In its legal sense, documentation and record keeping can be for the protection of the nurse or doctor who is part of the patient care.

A well-kept record can protect the practitioner in instances where a legal defence is necessary. Documentation also ensures proof and professionalisation of the improvement of practices.

Types of Record-Keeping Found in Healthcare:

- Hand-written records

- Computer-based systems (electronic)
- Some employers or organisations use a blend of both.

Different parts of a patient's records include:

- Medical records
- Nursing records/progress notes
- Medication charts
- Laboratory orders and reports
- Vital signs observation charts
- Handover admission and sheets
- Discharge and transfer checklists/ letters
- Patient's assessment forms, such as nutrition or pressure area care assessment.

Principles of Good Record Keeping

Some key factors underpin good record keeping. The patient's records should be as follows:

- It should be factual, accurate and steady;
- Updated after any recordable event immediately;
- Provide current information on the condition and care of the patient;
- Documented in such a way that the text cannot be erased easily;
- It should be consecutive, timed and dated accurately, and all entries signed (including any alterations);
- All original entries should be legible. Changes should be clear and noticeable with date and signature. It shouldn't include abbreviations, slang or jargon as not all workplaces or organisations use the same terminology absolutely;

- Records must be kept securely and should only be destroyed as per the local policy;
- Avoid meaningless phrases, speculations and offensive subjective statements/insulting or derogatory language;
- Identify the individual by recording patient's name, date of birth and hospital number on each page of the record (three approved identifiers) or follow your local policies on identification of patient's records;
- If photocopied or scanned It should be legible.

Common Deficiencies in Record Keeping:

- Poor record keeping hampers patient care and makes it difficult for healthcare professionals to guard their practice.

The most common zero record keeping include:

- Lack of clarity
- Inaccuracies
- Spelling mistakes
- Missing information
- Whenever a nagging problem has been detected.

Great things about Good Record Keeping

Record keeping is a tool for professional practice, and it is one which should help the patient care process. It is not something separate or optional to be fitted in if circumstances allow.

A record should be made as quickly as possible after the patient is seen or the task is complete. It's important that accurate records are created in the patient's file which should include interventions and any response to the interventions.

The need for a good record keeping are:

- Record keeping makes the continuity of care easier;
- Record keeping promotes better communication and dissemination of information between the members of the multi-professional team;
- Helps to address complaints or legal processes effectively;
- Supports clinical audit, research, allocation of performance and resources planning;
- Helps to identify risks and early detection of complications;
- Supports patient care and patient-centred communication;
- Supports effective clinical judgement;
- Supports delivery of services;
- Helps improve accountability;
- Shows decisions made related to patient's care.

Legal Issues in Record Keeping

- The patient's records are required as evidence before a court of law occasionally, or to investigate a complaint in a certain area, organisation level.
- Sometimes records could be requested by professional governing bodies when investigating claims linked to misconduct.
- It is therefore critical to keep up-to-date with the legal requirements and best practices of record-keeping, proving that:
- A comprehensive nursing assessment of the individual has been undertaken including care that is provided and planned;

- Relevant information is roofed as well as any actions that has been used in response to changes in patients' conditions;
- The duty of patient care t has been executed and no acts have been compromised towards patient's safety;
- Arrangements have been made for the continuity of care for the patient.

Paper Medical Record – Definition

Medical records are a mixture of self-reported patient information and clinical diagnostic notes traditionally kept on paper-based mediums.

Advantages of Paper Medical Records

1. **Reduced Upfront Costs :** With paper medical records, all you need, in order to get started is paper, files, and a locked cabinet to store the documents. Besides, you don't need considerable training programs to upskill nurses and doctors on the intricacies of managing electronic health systems. These costs are incurred during implementation of an EHR and during on boarding a new healthcare provider.
2. **Ease of Use in a Familiar Format:** There's a good reason why paper medical records were an industry's mainstay for a number of decades. It is simple to pull up information from a file, examine previous notes and medical charts, and record new observations.

   If the information is accurately written, there may be fewer issues in reading charts and notes while data recovery. incase of Software you should enter the right keywords and user ID to access data. Not everyone is tech-savvy and able to transition to a new technology easily.

3. **Physical Form Factor:** Electronic medical records sound great in writing (no pun intended) but what do you do when there's a crisis?

   When time is of the essence, such as multiple trauma victims requiring immediate action, slow loading time and unfamiliar interfaces may waste important minutes as nurses search for databases using keywords and scroll past various screens to access previous records.

   Paper records are far more beneficial in such a scenario: A physical file is with all previous charts and health records neatly sorted at a single location. Additionally, the facts can be passed on from one person to another seamlessly. Of course, all of this depends on the notes being neatly written ,meticulously organized , and readily accessible .

4. **Easier to Customize:** Another good thing about paper medical records is that it's easier to customize and execute the requirements as per the need of the hospital/doctor. Need a fresh template? Just design one on a typical text editor and you're all set.

   With electronic health records, however, you'll need a software developer to create adjustments to the code and back end systems. That's both frustrating and costly.

Disadvantages of the Paper Medical Records

1. **Storage isn't Scalable:** Unlike electronic medical records that can be kept on cloud servers, paper medical records need physical space for storage purposes.

A single cloud server could store thousands of patient medical records, but the same in physical files will require a lot of space. And it's not only about assigning an explicit room and stuffing files there- they are valuable repositories of data and require careful handling. Hence, you almost certainly need temperature-controlled rooms and other mechanisms to ensure data integrity.

2. **Insufficient Backups & Limited Security :** What now ? if there's a fire that wipes out your entire physical files? Or a moth infestation that, quite literally, eats up all of your data? Physical files, lost once, are impossible to recover. Electronic records, however, have data backup and storage, so even if a malicious entity manages to infiltrate and get access, there's a fallback option still.
3. **Frustrating & Error Prone:** Paper medical records necessitates manual written process which is both frustrating and error prone. If you've ever attempted to read a doctor's notes, you'll understand that the writing isn't always legible and hence it can be hard to interpret.

   An electronic system doesn't have these problems- records aren't handwritten, so the legibility issue does not arise at all. also you don't have to search for patient files in a physical cabinet - the software does that for you (instantly).
4. **Inconsistent Layouts:** While paper based records could be much better to customize, its layout and format of information could be inconsistent from one record to another. Electronic records have a regular format which healthcare providers can get accustomed to.

When paper based records have different layouts, it increases the time needed to get the (potentially life saving) information for a patient. With electronic records healthcare providers can get familiar with a few formats of data, which will reduce the time required to find and analyze information.

5. **No Clear Audit Trails & Version History:** Paper records do not have built-in audit trails and version history. To know the changes/additions/ edits made it requires that the physician signs the records every time a change is done. If the changes are created, it's not simple to trace where and who made the changes.
6. This is important when auditing records or trying to look for a previous physician who has added information. In such a scenario a component of human error is always possible. Electronic health records have versions and logs that simplify tracking and auditing by automating it.

Paper Vs. Electronic Medical Record Keeping

When it comes to deciding between paper vs. electronic records, there are many things that you need to take into consideration.

Electronic health records are far more secure than paper records as they're not at risk in a catastrophic event.

When it comes to retaining accountability in electronic health records are much better - here each entry log corresponds with a particular individual. This factor helps in keeping track of who is diagnosing patients and recommending medical outcomes.

Lastly, EHRs ship in a custom-made format that helps in matters like legibility and accuracy of medical data. Paper-based records can involve human error and loss of data integrity.

EMR vs EHR - What's the Difference?

Electronic medical records (EMRs) certainly are a digital version of the paper charts in the clinician's office. An EMR provides the medical and treatment history of the patients in the same setting. EMRs definitely have advantages over paper records.

For instance, EMRs allow clinicians to:

- Track data over a time
- Identify patients due for preventive checkups or screenings
- Check their patients progress on certain parameters such as blood pressure, vaccinations or other readings
- Monitor and improve overall quality of care within the practice

But the information in EMRs doesn't travel easily out of practice. In fact, the patient's record might even have to be printed out and delivered by mail to professionals and other members of the care team. In this regard EMRs aren't superior to a paper record.

Electronic health records (EHRs) do these things and more. EHRs give attention to the total health of the patient, going beyond standard clinical data collected in the provider's office including a broader take on a patient's care.

EHRs are created to reach out beyond the healthcare organization that collects and compiles the information. They are built to share information with other health care providers, such as laboratories and specialists, so that the information is disseminated to the multidisciplinary medical team involved in patient's care. The National Alliance for Health IT explained that EHR data "could be created, managed, and consulted by authorized clinicians and staff across multiple healthcare organizations."

The details move with the patient-to the specialist, a healthcare facility, the nursing home, to another state or even across the country in comparing the variations between record types.

"The EHR represents the ability to easily share medical information among stakeholders and have a patient's information follow him or her through the various modalities of care engaged by that individual." EHRs are designed to be accessed by all involved in patient's care-including the patients themselves. Indeed, that's an explicit expectation in the Stage 1 definition of "meaningful use" of EHRs.

And that makes all of the difference. Since information is shared in a secure way, more better. Health care is a united team effort, and shared information supports that effort. After all, much of the value derived from the health care delivery system results from the effective communication of information from one party to another and, ultimately, the ability of multiple parties to engage in interactive communication of information.

Benefits of EHRs

- With fully functional EHRs, team members have ready access to the latest information enabling more coordinated, patient-centered care. With EHRs:
- The facts gathered by the principal care provider tells the emergency department clinician about the patient's

life threatening allergy, in order that care could appropriately be adjusted, if the patient is unconscious or otherwise.

- A patient can log on to his/her own record and see the data over a period of time (eg: Lab reports) this can hugely motivate him/her to take medications and keep up or modify lifestyle accordingly..
- The latest lab results will be available in the record to tell the expert the status of the patient without having to run the duplicate tests.
- The clinician's notes from the patient's hospital stay can help in providing the discharge instructions and follow-up care. It also allows the patient to move from one care setting to another more smoothly.
- So, yes, the difference between "electronic medical records" and "electronic health records" is merely one word. But in that expressed word there is a world of difference.

How do you and your patients usually maintain the health records?

We bet, you keep up a file of all prescriptions, scans and tests, health screening reports, discharge summaries, and store it in a safe place.

However, there are numerous problems linked with maintaining physical health records:

- One of the major problems is that you have to be extremely organized to be able to make sure you keep the records in the same file in the same location every time you take it out. If not, they can never be found when you need them.

- Another nagging problem is that paper can deteriorate over the years. You may even wrap up losing a significant record which may prove costly for you.
- Carrying physical records with you whenever you travel can be extremely cumbersome!

With EHR, it is much much easier to maintain your entire health records in a single location rather than lose them again and again. Moreover, you have easier access to your medical records anytime, anywhere and from any place you want!

KNOWLEDGE BYTE 7

HOW CAN YOU AND YOUR PATIENTS GO FOR EHR?

Its Simple! Get yourself registered with an Electronic Health Records service provider.

Before registering with any Electronic Health Record service, please check the benefits or features it has.

In case of emergency your healthcare providers can access the same in an event allowed by you. You will have your complete health records, even if you have submitted all of the original documents at time of insurance claim.

List of Benefits/Features that ought to be in your Electronic Health Record providers:

- **Pocket-sized Lifesaving Identity Card:** Health records can be found even when there is no mobile.
- **Lifesaving Corporate Identity card:** To provide benefits associated with Electronic Health Records and Corporate identity card.

- **It should be cloud based:** Health records should be available 24/7 on Cloud based platforms.
- **Works on all platforms:** Stay linked from anywhere; there shouldn't be a need to buy a special device.
- **Simple Interface:** No need to be tech-savvy. It should be simple and user-friendly.
- **Completely secured:** It should have minimum 256 Bits data security (Equal to Bank transaction).
- **Brief Health History should be on patients health card:** By viewing patients Health card, anyone can have access to patients data such as Name, Address, Age, emergency contact details, blood group, Mini Health History (allergies, blood pressure, diabetes, Medical Health Insurance policy number and name etc.
- **Self-manageable Health card:** There is no need for Patients/Healthcare providers to approach the customer service team to update Health History.
- **Health records should be easily accessible by Healthcare Providers with complete privacy:** In case of emergency Health records are essential. The patients should have complete control over their documents and simultaneously it also should be easily accessible to the health care providers in case of emergency with their consent.

Conclusion

Digital Health records, as opposed to paper-based Health Records, are records where data is accessible to patients and not merely to the providers. Digital Health Records provide more advantages to patients, thanks to the ever increasing widespread access to the internet and mobile devices!

Patients now have access to health information via web or telecommunication devices such as mobile phones, personal digital assistants and tablet computers.

Digital Health Records have the potential to help patients. Healthcare providers can access medical prescriptions and patient conditions from multiple locations, which will minimize errors and help quicken the diagnosis during emergencies, especially when patients go to a new provider, or when paper-based records are not available.

Now get your patients registered free* for Electronic Health Records service by visiting-

MDHL – My Digital Health Locker (https://app.mdhl.in/)

Or

Download the MDHL – My Digital Health Locker mobile application from play store or app store.

How does it work?

Step 1: Register and Login with https://app.mdhl.in/get your unique MDHL ID

Step 2: Print your own Health Card [which will have your Name, Address, Age, Emergency contact details, Blood group, Mini Health History (allergies, blood pressure, diabetes….), Health Insurance policy name and number, etc., to carry your complete health records in your pocket/mobile.

Step 3: Upload all the records onto the secured digital Health Locker. In order to scan the documents, simply take a picture of them.

Or

Request your healthcare providers (or yourself) to Email all the health records to your unique MDHL ID.

Step 4: Approve the Health records (to avoid spams).

Step 5: Whenever you need to access your medical records online, sign in or merely enter your details to access them. You can view your personal health records online on the https://app.mdhl.in/

In case of emergency your healthcare providers can access the same if you permit(through OTP).

KNOWLEDGE BYTE 8

GREAT THINGS ABOUT DIGITAL MEDICAL PRACTICE

Digital medical practice will give you following benefits:

- You can attend more patient in less time
- As a result of predefined templates you can create a prescription in 2 minutes.
- You can create your own website, or Microsoft Excel workbook to formulate templates of prescriptions.
- You can also create a BSA based prescription template in excel to create error-free prescriptions.
- Whenever a patient books the appointment, they will get a reminder sms/email to avoid 'no-show' in the clinic.
- Opt for digital practice to store all the prescriptions to avoid medico-legal issues.

- Due to digital practice, medical practitioners can save time for issuing prescriptions.
- In digital practice 'there will be almost zero misinterpretation of the prescription'
- In case of emergency you can treat your existing patients effortlessly, as their complete health history is on your fingertips.

The road to good consumer care is complex and sophisticated, with multiple touch points and resources of data. Unlike other industries, the patient's customer journey is ongoing, instead of one time purchase or r experience. And, unlike other industries, the journey might literally mean life or death for the individual. For this reason, it is critical to build a long-term, loyal relationship with each consumer.

Today almost every industry must address "the Amazon effect": The expectation by consumers that they will receive the same level of personalization and utmost contact that they enjoy with online retailer Amazon. This is especially important at a time when Baby Boomers have become more tech savvy and demanding. They are spending out of pocket with high-deductible plans, and more possibilities for routine care from nontraditional sources.

The effect? They are picky. This generation of patients isn't ready to spend time on traditional processes and paperwork; they need immediate access to doctors, lab results, and contact centers. Much like Amazon, they need price transparency and supporting data to help them make healthcare decisions. They expect a familiar level of convenience similar to what is available in retail and banking, and use social media to make the facility known to everyone.

Such expectations might offer new opportunities for healthcare operators. For instance, eRx offers intelligent contact center and real-time communication solutions which create a far more patient-centric method of healthcare. They facilitate access to medical care from any device and offer collaboration tools that support voice, video, and document sharing. With these tools, the provider achieves a 360-degree view of the patient in real time, and the patient receives an overall omni channel experience.

Digital transformation also moves patient care to a new level of information and intimacy.

By fueling more progressive approaches to care, these new activities are evolving patient expectations to the next level and realizing the dream of care anywhere, anytime.

Digitization has the potential to affect every aspect of care delivery and operations, enabling smarter choices and better utilization of time and resources and allowing individuals to spend additional time on patient interaction at the idea of care.

"Digital Practice can boost the individual experience, increase patient engagement and improve practice efficiency."

Knowledge Byte 9

PRECAUTIONS TO BE TAKEN, IF YOU PLAN FOR DIGITAL MEDICAL PRACTICE

Following points to be checked before you opt for Digital practice:

1. Software/website should be user-friendly.
2. It should be mobile/tablet friendly.
3. You should be able to manage your complete medical practice through your mobile
4. Each medical practitioner should have their own website. This will help you in reaching out to the masses and your patients cannot view your competitor's details.
5. Your website must be customizable and less dependent on a software developer/service provider.
6. The software should have the facility to update the day to day happenings like add/modify/delete information.
7. It should have the facility to book/edit/delete appointments.

8. It should have the provision for sms and email confirmation of the appointment as well as reminder of the same on autopilot mode. This will reduce the number of 'no show' patients to great extent..
9. It should have the feature for payment collection and its statistics.
10. The software should be able to help you to access all the prescriptions and health history of the patients created by you to prevent medico-legal issues.
11. It should allow the diagnostic/pathology test template to save time.
12. It should have a minimum 256 bits security. (Equivalent to bank transaction)
13. Data transfer should be done through end-to-end encryption which means with complete security.
14. It should have an Auto-backup facility.
15. Software should have a 'prescription auto forward' facility through email.
16. It should have an inbuilt Drug-Drug interaction database.
17. Software should follow the ideal prescription format as suggested by the Medical Council.
18. It should permit 'unlimited prescription template', create any prescription, even BSA based in 2 minutes
19. All your data should be secured and be accessible only to you .
20. Domain name should have an SSL certificate. So, you are free from hackers.
21. It should incorporate an updated version of ICD. i.e. ICD 10.
22. It should have a reception module. So, your receptionist can also manage appointments.

CONCLUSION: POWER RECAP

In this book you have learnt:

- What particularly are the rules to create Ideal and Error-free Prescription?
- Some DOs and Don'ts for issuing the Prescription
- Points to be remembered when Verbal Prescription are issued
- Importance of Drug - drug interaction
- What's ICD - 10 and its own benefits?
- Maintaining Health records by you as well as your patients
- How can you and your patients go for EHR?
- Great things about Digital Medical Practice
- Precautions to be taken, If you plan for Digital Medical Practice

Let's join hands to digitize healthcare for humankind.

"Together with tens of hundreds of patients declining every year from preventable medical errors, it truly is imperative that we embrace available systems and drastically enhance the way medical information is handled and processed."

NOW, YOU HAVE TWO CHOICES

While you may have reached the end of this book, your work has just begun. Now comes the hard part. It's time to implement what you've learned in order to create a Digital Medical Oncologists Practice program that delivers significant, measurable results in your quality of service or to further strengthen a program that is already helping you to provide high-quality, cost effective care.

After all, even a small improvement can have a significant impact on the patient experience. Steadily you can keep working to achieve bigger enhancements and see their effect on an even larger portion of your patient population. By maintaining an unwavering commitment to the building blocks of care management — a team-based, patient-centered approach to care — and a desire to truly transform your delivery of care, you will be surprised to know how quickly your efforts begin to positively impact the lives of your patient populations.

1. Conquer every roadblock and do it yourself. For this You need to hire a developer for initial set up and maintenance. later an assistant can work through these complex applications. For instance, Initial

cost will be Rs.1,50,000/- for website development. Annual recurring cost will be Rs.1000/- for domain, Rs.10,000/- for web hosting service, Rs.3,000 for SSL For website, Rs.3,000/- For Email service, Rs.5,000/- for email auto responder (remind appointment through email) Rs.2000/- for transactional SMS (remind appointment through SMS), Rs.10,000/- for Website Maintenance. Total cost can go up to Rs.1,84,000 for first year and then Rs.34,000/year for subsequent years.

2. Have your own Digital Medical Practice through eRx with almost negligible costing, compared to having your own and making sure you are doing right. Basically, blast through the roadblocks and see your medical practice getting enhanced so that you attend more patients in less time and earn more profits.

CALL TO ACTION

Don't wait to Roar your medical Oncologist Practice. Visit now and Register immediately through the link below:

https://www.erx.co.in/commoncontrols/login.aspx

Sources

https://www.maharashtramedicalcouncil.in/

https://nabh.co/Images/PDF/SOPs/MANAGEMENT_OF_MEDICATION.pdf

https://en.wikipedia.org/

www.ingramcontent.com/pod-product-compliance
Ingram Content Group UK Ltd.
Pitfield, Milton Keynes, MK11 3LW, UK
UKHW021654190726
13853UKWH00001B/262

9 789391 266158